Y0-BLD-263

American Economic History

The Real World Books

AMERICAN ECONOMIC HISTORY

ECONOMICS OF THE CONSUMER

THE ECONOMICS OF
   UNDERDEVELOPED COUNTRIES

HOW A MARKET ECONOMY WORKS

INTERNATIONAL TRADE

THE LABOR MOVEMENT IN
   THE UNITED STATES

THE LAW AND ECONOMICS

MODERN TRADE UNIONISM

MONEY AND BANKING

THE STOCK MARKET

TAXES

We specialize in producing quality books for young people. For a complete list please write

LERNER PUBLICATIONS COMPANY
241 First Avenue North, Minneapolis, Minnesota 55401

the real world series

American Economic History

Kenneth H. Smith

Associate Professor of Economics
Hunter College, City University of New York

Editorial Consultant: Marc Rosenblum

Lerner Publications Company—Minneapolis, Minnesota

ACKNOWLEDGMENTS

The illustrations are reproduced through the courtesy of: pp. 8, 99, National Aeronautics and Space Administration; pp. 12, 88-89, United Nations; pp. 13, 65, International Harvester Company; p. 18, National Maritime Museum, Greenwich, England; pp. 21, 25, 45, 60, 71, 75, 96, Independent Picture Service; pp. 23, 26-27, 32-33, 42-43, 48, 56-57, Library of Congress; p. 29, Virginia State Library; p. 37, The Virginia Museum of Fine Arts; p. 47, Kennedy Galleries, Inc.; pp. 52-53, National Archives, United States Signal Corps Photograph; p. 59, Standard Oil Company; p. 64, Chase Manhattan Bank Money Museum; p. 67, Chicago Historical Society; p. 69, Educational Affairs Department, Ford Motor Company; p. 76, National Archives, United States Office of War Information; p. 79, Ewing Galloway, New York; p. 81, Franklin D. Roosevelt Library (Wide World Photo); p. 90, National Archives, United States Information Agency; p. 94, Ford Motor Company; p. 97, United States Army Photograph.

Copyright © 1970 by Lerner Publications Company

All rights reserved. International copyright secured. Manufactured in the United States of America. Published simultaneously in Canada by J. M. Dent & Sons Ltd., Don Mills, Ontario.

International Standard Book Number: 0-8225-0612-2
Library of Congress Catalog Card Number: 75-84415

Second Printing 1972

Contents

1 Principles of Economic History — 7

2 European Beginnings: The Institutional Heritage — 14

3 The Beginnings of Economic Growth — 19

4 The Political Foundations of Growth — 35

5 Building a National Economy: 1789-1865 — 40

6 Industrialization, Growth, and Instability: 1866-1929 — 54

7 Development of American Capitalism: 1929 to the Present — 78

Glossary — 101

Index — 102

If history teaches us anything, it is this lesson: So far as the economic potential of our nation is concerned, the believers in the future of America have always been the realists.

DWIGHT D. EISENHOWER

1

Principles of Economic History

Our present civilization is a mixture of many aspects of life — social, political, cultural, religious, and economic. The present is also the stepping-stone between the past and future. The purpose of history is to gather all the facts about the past and weave them together to explain the development of modern civilization.

Too many facts, however, may be confusing. To better interpret the whole of human history it is necessary to examine its parts separately and in detail before assembling a broad overview. Thus some historians have concentrated on political or social events; others have focused attention on the pattern of economic development.

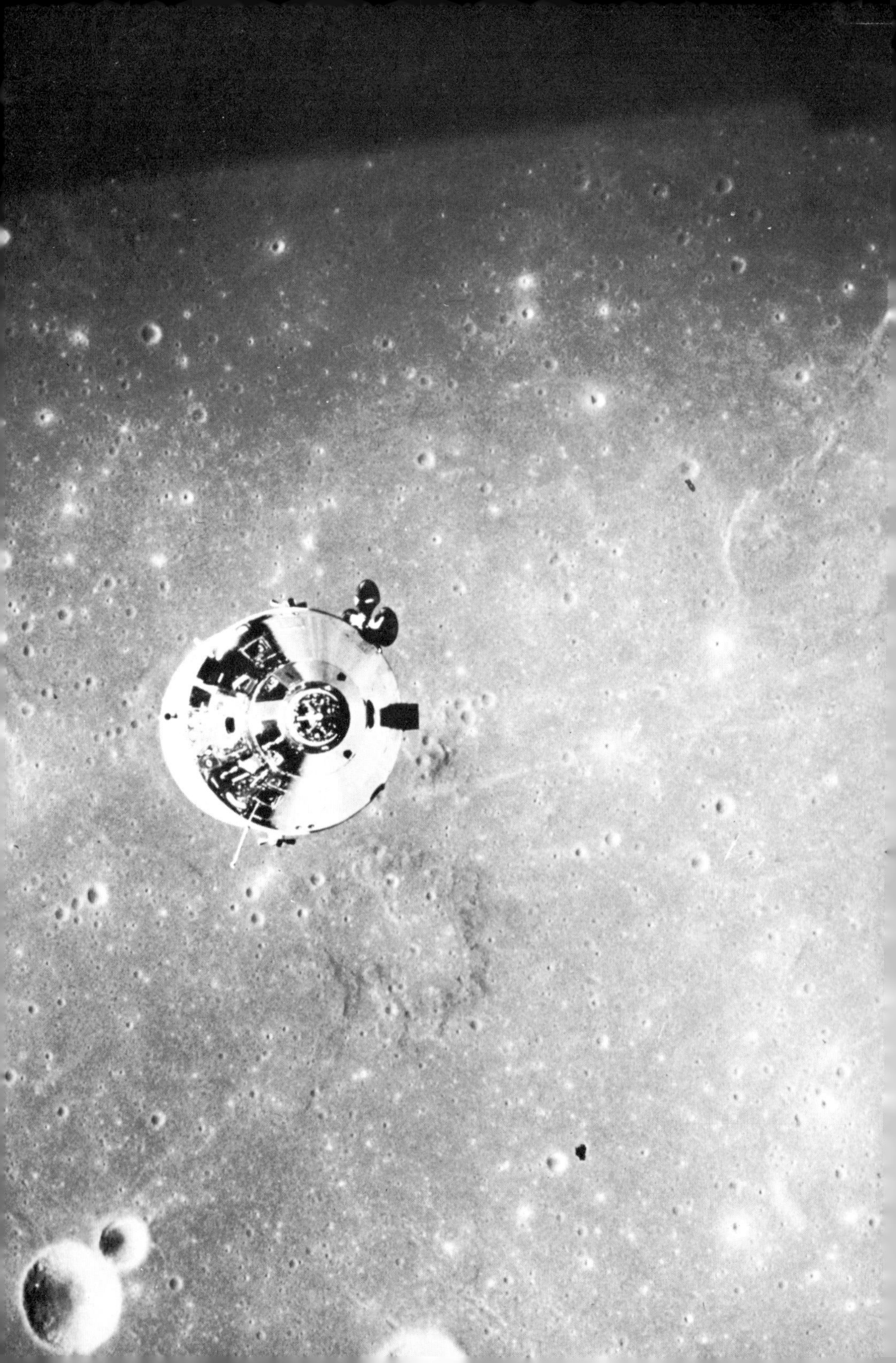

Left: The Apollo 11 Command Module, photographed from the Lunar Module, as it was leaving to take men to the moon for the first time. In less than 200 years the United States has become an industrial economy able to undertake the exploration of space.

Economic history has been a field of special interest for over 100 years, but it has gained new importance since World War II. Developing nations have sought to find in the past the factors which have led to economic progress elsewhere; more advanced economies have been interested in learning how to increase their growth rates. To avoid repeating failures and to benefit from past experience, policy makers have increasingly asked questions that can only be answered by economic history.

Traditionally, economic historians have collected facts describing how man has satisfied his material needs. They have studied the kinds of goods and services man used, the ways they were produced, and the institutions and organizations employed to distribute them.

To understand this process, modern historians have found it necessary to consider the influence of government economic policies on the way man makes his living, and also to examine changes in income and in patterns of production. From this record it is possible to show what combinations of factors have led to economic development and growth.

Economic history does not provide a foolproof formula for growth and prosperity, but it does single out the key factors which have brought change, and it shows how certain economic policies will work under various conditions. It also furnishes an analysis of what has happened, so that we may attempt to repeat or avoid specific events.

The economic history of the United States has been of special interest not only in this country, but also throughout the world. What has made it possible for the United States to achieve the greatest productivity and the highest standard of living in the world? Why was it first to send men to land on the moon? How has an economy become so wealthy that it can afford to start a program to eliminate poverty when most nations would be satisfied with an average income half that of the United States? Merely presenting economic facts from the past cannot answer these questions. The job of economic history is to apply the concepts of economic theory to historical facts, to select the most important conditions and explain how they interacted to create the development that occurred.

The first condition with which the economic historian is concerned is physical environment: What is the country's geographic location, climate, and size? What are its natural resources — minerals, forests, water, and quality of land? Next he looks at the human resources, as a labor force and also as consumers: How large is the population? What part of it is able to work? What are the skills and education levels? How efficient, how productive are the people?

A third consideration is the economy's *capital* (equipment with which labor works and the money which buys it): How much capital does the country have? How fast does new capital become available? Not the least important to the historian is *entrepreneurship*, the individuals and the institutions that exist to put the factors of production into operation: Are there strong desires to work hard and gain material wealth? Is there a willingness to take risks and an ability to analyze economic conditions? Is success measured by achievement? Do political and social organizations encourage change and adapt quickly to it?

Finally, the economic historian is concerned with a country's *technology:* How advanced are the methods of production? What is the main source of energy — manpower, oxen, or steam turbines? How rapid is the flow of new inventions and how soon are they actually put to use? What effect does the kind and amount of technology have on the output of economic goods and services?

Answers to these questions provide the economic historian with the facts he needs in order to interpret the past operation and the development of an economy. He then analyzes this information in terms of supply and demand. Under the heading of *supply*, the economist includes the resources of land, labor, capital, entrepreneurship, and technology in an economy. These can be matched with *demand* factors — size of the population to be served, the level of income and its relative purchasing power, the need for investment by business, and the amount of government

A country's technology is an important factor affecting its economic growth. Many underdeveloped countries, such as Ethiopia, do not have the production methods to use their resources efficiently.

purchases, as well as the demand abroad for an economy's exports.

How nearly supply and demand equal each other shows the economic historian the efficiency of the economy at a particular stage in its development. An economy operates at the highest level of efficiency when supply and demand are equal. The relationship between supply and demand over periods of time indicates whether the economy is growing, standing still, or slowing down. In the Great Depression (1929-1939), for example, the supply from the factors of production was much greater than the demand from citizens and government. This caused a recession, or slowing down, in the United States economy.

The amount of information concerning the economic history of even a part of an economy — an industry or a region, for example — can be very large. From detailed accounts a broad survey of events must be constructed, emphasizing the direction and the rate of economic development. The following chapters describe American economic progress within this framework.

Countries which use advanced methods of production can make more efficient use of their resources and thus develop more rapidly.

2

European Beginnings: The Institutional Heritage

Development of the American continents had to wait for the necessary political, social, philosophical, and technical progress in Europe. The three centuries before the first permanent settlement at Jamestown, Virginia, in 1607 ushered in a series of significant events that made colonization possible.

The rise of the market system and the evolution of commercial capitalism from feudalism in Europe was the first of these changes. During the Middle Ages much of Europe was divided into estates owned and ruled by feudal overlords. A feudal estate, or fief, was like a small kingdom; it produced everything it needed. Thus under the feudal system there was not much trade or commerce. Commerce and industry began to develop in the fourteenth century. Merchants and businessmen gradually replaced feudal landowners in importance and power. Free enterprise was developed; the means of production were owned privately and used for private profit without government interference.

One part of feudalism itself was important in the colonization of the Americas, the concept of private property. Feudalism had placed a high value on real estate; land was the principal measure of wealth. The feudal system of laws set up a system for ownership and transfer of land, and laid out the obligations of the contracting parties. These arrangements were brought to the New World.

The Protestant Reformation (a split from the Roman Catholic Church in the sixteenth century) was also an important change. Protestantism tended to turn people's attention to their welfare in this world, emphasized hard work as a positive virtue, and accepted business activity as a moral calling. The Reformation provided a philosophical basis for a greater interest in obtaining economic goods.

Scientific experimentation and discovery aided the colonization of the Americas. The astrolabe (an instrument used to determine a ship's position at sea), improved compasses and other navigation aids, and the caravel (the first fast and dependable ocean-going vessel), were all in use before 1600.

Methods of trade and business had to be developed before colonization was possible. Banking techniques, accounting systems, and commercial trading centers evolved as trade expanded. The founding of joint stock companies was also important for colonization because it made raising the required large sums of money easier. (A joint stock company had many contributors, who shared the cost of investment in overseas development and shared all profits or losses.)

Political developments during this time were also important. Out of the patchwork of feudal estates, new nations took form. Britain became England. Across the English Channel, Philip Augustus annexed fief after fief and formed France. The many small kingdoms on the Iberian peninsula became Spain and Portugal.

Leaders of these new nations required the support of the landholding classes to maintain their power. In order to balance the influence of the landowners and at the same time increase the wealth of their respective countries, kings encouraged the growing class of merchants and traders. Within the new countries trade and commerce enjoyed a revival; travelers and traders had greater protection, there were fewer trade barriers, and private local warfare decreased.

The traditional trade of Western Europe had been centered around the Mediterranean Sea. It was the shortest route to the East and the most familiar. It was used in the days of the Romans, and even by traders of the Greek and Egyptian empires. The Mediterranean trade routes had been closed in the fourteenth century by the Ottoman Turks, who controlled much of the Mediterranean until the sixteenth century.

Because of the Turkish dominance, new trade routes to the East were necessary if European nations were to prosper. Thus merchants, explorers, and adventurers, under the sponsorship of their monarchs, began an era of discovery and colonization in Africa and in the Western Hemisphere.

Exploration and colonization were part of the economic policy of *mercantilism*, which influenced many European nations from the sixteenth through the eighteenth centuries. The mercantilists favored building the wealth of a nation through a "favorable balance of trade" (having more exports than imports). This trade surplus would fill the treasury with gold, silver, precious metals, and gems.

Mercantilism sought not only to develop export

A Spanish galleon (left) carrying silver from Peru is captured by a British ship. Spain and England, like many mercantilistic countries in the sixteenth through eighteenth centuries, tried to obtain as much gold and silver as possible. This sometimes led to piracy.

trade, but also to seek colonies which might be a source of gold and silver. Spain and Portugal succeeded in establishing mineral-producing colonies in Mexico, Peru, and Brazil. Colonies provided other raw materials not available in the mother country and served as markets for her finished products. The mercantilists recommended that governments should encourage colonization by financing joint stock companies, by giving trade companies exclusive charters (monopolies) to establish and settle colonies, and by building a strong navy to protect commerce on the seas and in foreign countries.

By the 1600s, then, conditions in Europe were ready for the colonization and development of the great continents lying to the west.

3

The Beginnings of Economic Growth

The early settlements in North America were along the Atlantic coast, near good seaports and broad rivers flowing inland — the Hudson, Connecticut, Susquehanna, Delaware, and James. These waterways provided transportation to the interior, and the coastal towns became trading centers for inland regions. The favorable natural setting of the American settlements included ocean currents and trade winds which aided foreign commerce.

The climate along the Atlantic coast was much like that of Europe. The temperature averaged between 40 and 70 degrees annually; rainfall was 30 to 50 inches a year (20 inches is considered the essential minimum for agriculture). Although the climate was different in the northern and southern settlements, climatic conditions were almost ideal in both.

Right: A feudal castle and village. Under the feudal system, each farmer had strips of land to work. In the fifteenth and sixteenth centuries, landholders dismissed their farmers and began to raise cash crops or sheep. Many of the farmers came to North America to begin a new life.

Central North America also offered settlers a wide range of soil and minerals. The area just east of the Appalachian Mountains contained good sandy loam, and also rich river bottoms. This area also had many forests, and wood for fuel and housing was important to colonial existence. Minerals necessary to the production of gunpowder, iron, glass, paper, and brick were also present.

Animal life and fish were plentiful, as were a number of wild plants and fruits. The Indians cultivated many of them and shared their knowledge with the settlers. Native crops of maize (Indian corn), pumpkins, squash, beans, tomatoes, peanuts, watermelons, and huckleberries were all part of the colonists' diet.

Shortage of Labor and Capital

An analysis of the colonies in the economic framework of supply and demand shows that supply factors were much greater than demand factors, especially population. Under these conditions, an economy can experience some economic development, but it cannot develop very rapidly. Although America was rich in natural resources, human labor to use and develop them was relatively scarce for more than 250 years after the first settlements. The tremendous economic growth which the United States later experienced was not possible until the demand for the abundant supply of resources more nearly equaled the supply. The size of the population, an important demand factor, grew in two ways: America received a constant flow of immigrants, and it maintained a high birth rate.

At first a desire for gold and silver caused emigration to the colonies. Only after several years did men realize that the true wealth to be gained in the New World was land. Real property had long been a symbol of wealth and position in Europe, where it was also the primary means of livelihood. Land ownership came about by inheritance or through purchase at a very high price, and consequently most of the population did not own land. A majority of the population farmed land belonging to a feudal lord.

Right: A quilting bee in Virginia. To make up for a shortage of workers, settlers joined together in many projects.

Feudalism began to decline in the fourteenth century, and landowners began to dismiss their farmers as they found more profitable ways to manage their holdings. Because of increased industrialization and commerce the feudal manor no longer had to produce everything it needed. Many farmers were let go as landholders began to raise cash crops instead of what was needed for self-sufficiency of the manor.

Development of the textile industry in England raised the price of wool, which made sheep raising more profitable than agriculture. Many English landowners in the sixteenth and seventeenth centuries began to use their fields as pasture for sheep, forcing many farm workers to seek employment elsewhere. Some found jobs in the cities, but many became beggars and vagabonds.

Partly because the young industries were not able to hire all of the farmers who were without work, and also because of the promotional activity of the various trading companies who promised settlers free land, a steady flow of immigrants to America began. Most of the immigrants were of English stock, but 20 to 40 percent were Irish, German, Dutch, Scottish, and Scandinavian.

During the early years of development the North American population grew rapidly. Although accurate census data is not available, it is estimated, from written accounts, tax rolls, and church records, that in 170 years colonial population grew from 200 (the original settlers of Virginia) to almost two and a quarter million. Population of the colonies doubled every 20 to 25 years.

Although immigration played a large role in the population increase, the greatest increase in population after 1650 was due to the high birth rate. Colonists married earlier, had more children, and (because of better diet) enjoyed a longer life span than the Europeans.

Even with this population growth, labor was in short supply. The settlers compensated for the shortage of workers by raising large families and working long hours. They also pooled their labor in barn-raisings, harvesting, and quilting bees.

Right: The first Negro slaves are brought to Jamestown, Virginia, in 1619. The slave trade was declared illegal in the United States in 1808.

The use of *indentured servants* supplemented the settlers' cooperative efforts. These non-free workers were of two classes — voluntary and involuntary. Many individuals entered into an indentured contract of their own free will. They promised to work usually four to seven years in exchange for ship passage to the colonies, and food, clothing, and shelter during their service. Most importantly, they were given a parcel of land at the completion of the agreed period of time. In New Jersey an indentured servant might receive as much as 75 acres. He would receive 50 acres in Maryland, where over 5,000 indentured persons entered the colony between 1670 and 1678.

Other indentured servants were sent to the colonies involuntarily. These were usually debtors, vagrants, or criminals sent out of the country by the English courts; thus they were called "His Majesty's Seven-Year Passengers."

Most of the labor of the northern colonies was free or indentured, but the middle and southern colonies used many slaves. The first Negro slaves were sold at Jamestown by a Dutch merchant in 1619. The slave trade was begun in the 1480s by Portuguese traders who carried slaves to Europe from the west coast of Africa, and it lasted about 400 years. In spite of the continuing labor shortage, slave labor was unpopular in the American colonies and grew slowly. The traffic in slaves increased after 1689 as

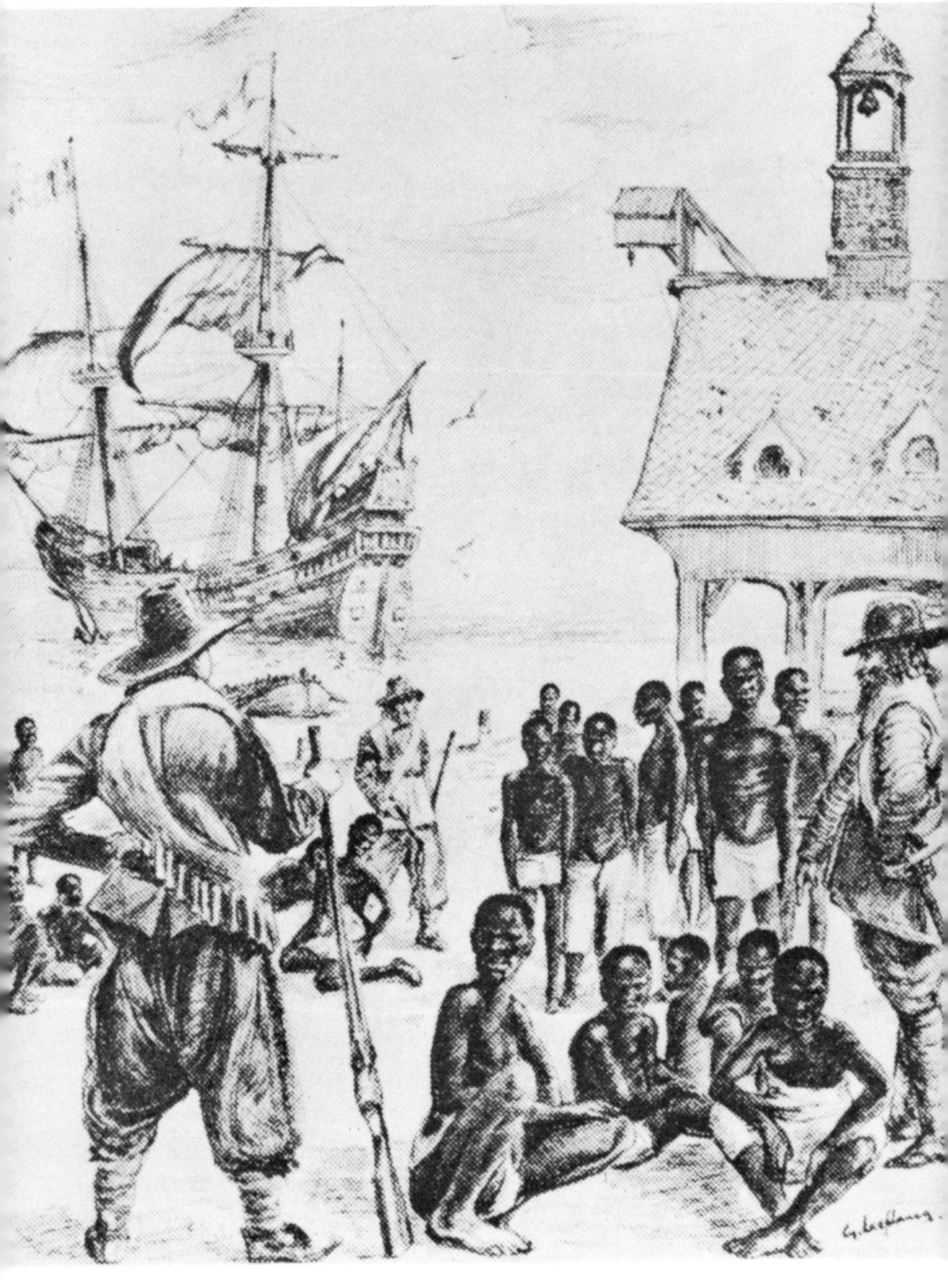

The first day at Jamestown, Virginia. Wealthy men (left) refuse to work. They had come to North America hoping for easy riches. On the right are indentured servants clearing the land.

tobacco and rice plantations expanded, but it was on a sharp decline at the time of the Revolutionary War. The invention of the cotton gin in 1793, however, made raising cotton profitable, and slave traffic was revived.

Skilled labor was at a premium in the colonies. Wages in colonial America were generally higher than those in the Old World; skilled workers and artisans were able to earn two or three times the pay of their European counterparts. Some communities paid craftsmen and professionals bounties for locating with them. Craftsmen in a few areas were able to get

Right: A drawing on a map of Virginia and Maryland, 1775. The artist shows barrels of tobacco being prepared for shipment to Europe. Tobacco was one of the important cash crops in the colonies.

higher wages by organizing (forming unions). Most historians agree that colonial industry and manufacturing would have grown more rapidly if there had been a greater supply of skilled workers.

Capital was also scarce in the colonies. Since no precious metals had been discovered, there was a shortage of specie (coined money) which lasted until after the revolution. Barter (the direct exchange of goods, using no money) and commodity money (the use of a product, such as fur or rice, as legal tender) helped close the gap, but the main sources of money capital were credit supplied by merchants and paper currency. Productive capital (tools, machines, livestock, and industrial capital equipment) was entirely imported at first.

Economic Activity of the Colonies

Most of the economic activity in the colonial period of development centered around agriculture and foreign trade. Until 1890 more Americans made a living by farming than by any other occupation. This reflected the abundance of land, the efficiency of agricultural production, and the shortage of capital and skilled labor which is required for industry. American agriculture was largely self-sufficient soon after the first settlement, and thereafter produced a surplus to be sold to other colonists and overseas.

New England produced corn, wheat, barley, livestock, and many vegetables and fruits. The middle colonies — New Jersey, Pennsylvania, Maryland, and Delaware — were known as the "Bread Colonies" because of their grain output. But they also raised flax, tobacco, farm animals, and an even wider variety of fruits, berries, and vegetables than their northern neighbors. Southern farmers and planters raised food for their own use, but they concentrated on a few major commercial crops — tobacco, corn, rice, and indigo. Some colonists attempted to grow silkworms, figs, olives, and similar tropical products not grown in other English colonies, but they were unsuccessful.

The large-scale farms in the southern colonies, which used many slaves and indentured servants, were the first evidence of specialization (concentration on one or more products) in the American economy. These farms provided most of the exports necessary to get farm tools, pots, pans, tea, ammunition, and manufactured goods from abroad. The commercial crops were subject to price fluctuations (changes) which brought the southern colonies alternating periods of prosperity and depression.

Although colonial agricultural goods were mostly consumed locally, there was always enough surplus to supply the urban population and the export markets. This additional output was used as a substitute for money; it was traded for nonagricultural goods.

One of the keys to the solid economic base of the United States is that the population was able to raise the standard of living above the subsistence level at a very early stage. The colonists produced more than they required for survival, and they had enough surplus to exchange for the resources needed for growth — capital and technology.

This exchange of agricultural products for manufactured goods developed into a thriving international trade, the second most important economic activity of the colonies. Colonial merchants ignored the British Navigation Acts, which attempted to control all colonial exports and imports, and traded in the West Indies, Africa, and southern Europe.

Many colonial products were not needed in Europe. In order to pay for European goods, Americans exchanged their agricultural products and raw materials for items which were not available in Europe. Traders shipped fish, grain, lumber, naval stores, and meat to the Caribbean Islands and brought back molasses, money, fruit, rum, and sugar. These in turn were exchanged for manufactured goods from Europe or slaves from Africa.

The northern colonies had a continuing unfavorable balance of trade with the mother country; they imported more from England than they exported there. They therefore usually owed English creditors for long term and short term capital loans. Exports of the middle and southern colonies, along with the West Indian and African trade, however, kept the overall trade position in balance.

Fishing, forestry, and minor manufacturing industries were other economic activities in the colonies. The shipbuilding and food-processing industries made considerable progress, as did building construction and the manufacture of simple farm tools. The growth of trade required the development of business techniques — banking, insurance, advertising.

Economic Independence

The colonists brought to America the institutions and technology of Europe; they used the then best known methods of agricultural production and

Shipbuilding at East Boston. One of the earliest industries in New England was shipbuilding. It developed because of the importance of foreign trade and the abundance of timber.

economic organization. They also learned from the Indians and from their own experiences, bringing to bear the most efficient technology of the time on a nearly untouched continent.

The settlers themselves were hardy and ambitious. They had dared a dangerous ocean journey to an unknown land peopled with hostile Indians. Settlement was a matter of physical survival. The lack of craftsmen forced people to experiment, invent, and literally become jacks-of-all-trades in order to exist. The challenge of the environment drew from the colonists their own strongest resources to add to those of the New World.

In spite of various restrictions on the economy, such as the Navigation Acts, the colonies grew and prospered. By the end of the French and Indian War in 1763, they had formed their own elective assemblies, won certain rights from the governors, and begun to control most of their internal affairs. They were almost completely independent in economic matters.

After 150 years of neglect, England began to place political and economic controls on her colonies. She stationed troops there and required the colonies to house them. To help reduce England's national debt, and to pay for the soldiers, the English Parliament imposed new and higher taxes and placed new restrictions on trade and shipping. Hoping to end warfare with the Indians, England closed off western lands to colonial settlement. These measures, added to a period of depression, hit hard at the merchants and farmers and caused unrest in the colonies.

In the years since the first English settlement, new generations of Americans had grown up with a loyalty to their own land. They were independent, energetic, and self-reliant. Over one-fourth of the population was of non-English origin, much of it actually hostile to Great Britain. The colonies wanted freedom to trade overseas and to industrialize, and this was in genuine conflict of interest with England. Consequently, when England exerted its long-unused political and economic authority on the colonies, the result was revolution.

4

The Political Foundations of Growth

The United States suffered very little from the effects of the Revolutionary War. Although the conflict did cause some shortages of manufactured goods and food, this was the result of interrupted internal transportation and naval blockade, rather than a slacking off of production. A loss of manpower, as farmers were called to fight, did reduce the output of some agricultural products. Lack of tax revenues and large issues of paper money made the war difficult to finance and brought on serious inflation. American industry, however, actually benefited from the war, supplying arms, uniforms, boots, and military supplies to the Continental Army. Foreign aid and assistance from the French, Dutch, and to a lesser degree, the Spanish, provided credit, men, and supplies.

The war was a long distance from home, and consequently many English people were not interested in it. The English army used poor military strategy, whereas the colonists were led by a superior general, George Washington. Faced with fighting a guerilla war against determined men defending their homeland, the English forces met defeat.

The Articles of Confederation

The immediate postwar period marked the end of all British economic and political controls. Under the Articles of Confederation, the new plan of government, there was general agricultural expansion and a short period of prosperity.

The Articles established a central government which controlled the country's foreign affairs but had little power over the economy; it could not pass laws or impose taxes. These weaknesses limited the economic development of the new country. The states attempted to reduce their own war debts individually by levying heavy personal taxes. They restricted interstate trade by enacting import duties.

A drop in farm prices, competition from foreign imports, and conflicts over paper money issued by

The Constitutional Convention — Philadelphia, 1787. The delegates had planned to revise the weak Articles of Confederation; instead, they drew up a new plan of government. The Constitution provided a framework for the growth of capitalism.

individual states led to general dissatisfaction with the Articles of Confederation. A majority of citizens wanted a national government strong enough to protect manufacturing, create a sound currency, and aid business and commerce. These conditions led to a calling of a convention which wrote a new constitution.

The Constitution

The new plan of government provided a legal and political framework for the growth of capitalism. The federal government was given broad powers: it could levy taxes and control the currency; it could also establish tariffs for international trade. The Constitution eliminated all tariffs and trade duties between states. It protected private property and provided for the enforcing of contracts between individuals or businesses. The Constitution also included provisions for amendment, so that it would be able to adjust to future change. The Bill of Rights, added in 1791, guaranteed individual liberty, and it provided that no person would be deprived of his life or possessions without due process of law.

At the time the Constitution was ratified, the American economy was much stronger than it had been before the Revolutionary War. Commerce and trade within the country expanded. Manufacturing output was greater, and farm production continued to yield surpluses. Lack of capital goods and skilled labor, however, still limited the rate of growth. American products received more competition overseas, because the United States no longer had special trading privileges from the British empire. But the economic foundations of the country were strong and firmly established; the institutions and political structure for a market system were operating. Most importantly, the prime ingredients for growth were present.

From this base the United States economy began to evolve, each part — agriculture, manufacturing, labor force, capital, resources, commerce, foreign trade and technology — a partner to the change. Any one of these areas of the economy can be examined alone to discover the fascinating contribution it made to development, but in a brief treatment of economic history it is only possible to single out the most significant sources of change. It must be remembered that these few factors alone did not bring about the evolution of the economy; interacting with others, they did characterize the particular stage of development and largely determined its direction of thrust.

5

Building a National Economy: 1789-1865

The greatest influence on American economic development from 1789 to 1865 was a tremendous territorial expansion. Obtaining new territory stimulates growth and development as land is settled and exploited. New territory also creates a large market. Thus new territory brings a greater demand for goods and services and also a greater supply of resources to satisfy them: large increases in both supply and demand brought considerable economic progress to the United States.

The Louisiana Purchase, the annexation of Texas, the Mexican Cession, the Oregon Treaty, and the Gadsden Purchase filled out the United States to its present continental boundaries, creating a country stretching from the Atlantic to the Pacific Ocean. Huge supplies of natural resources and millions of acres of land came under United States control.

The rapidly increasing population, swelled by waves of immigration averaging over 200,000 per year after 1845, furnished a labor supply for agriculture, construction, and growing industries. Government land policies (which sold and granted land to individuals and the railroads), American daring, and improved transportation drew a third of the more than 35 million American citizens west of the Mississippi before the Civil War.

Transportation and Unification

As the American frontier moved westward to the Pacific the United States developed a single interdependent economy. The eastern and western markets were joined together first with roads, canals, and railroads, and then with the instant communication of the telegraph.

A drive for better roads came as a result of the desire of the states to be able to carry freight and passengers easily and cheaply. After the War of 1812, the federal government sponsored the National Road, a turnpike built from Cumberland, Maryland, west to Vandalia, Illinois. This route opened up the Ohio River valley for settlement and was so well engineered that much of it is used for highways today.

Congress failed to pursue the program of road-building, and private companies began to construct toll roads. State governments joined the efforts, and by 1830 New England and the middle Atlantic states had a fairly complete system of free and toll roads. The private ventures lost money, however, due to mismanagement and poor construction, and roads continued to be an expensive method of moving cargo.

The turnpike era came to an end with the revival of water transportation. Navigable rivers had long been the major means of commercial travel. The steam riverboat, first built by Robert Fulton in 1807,

The town of Lockport, New York, on the Erie Canal. The canal linked Albany, on the Hudson River, with Buffalo, on Lake Erie. Canals gave inland regions a way to trade with other parts of the growing economy.

cut freight costs and made upstream trips with heavy cargo possible. The river system, the intercoastal waterways, and the Great Lakes became means of tying together local markets east of the Mississippi with relatively cheap, dependable transportation.

The completion of the Erie Canal in 1825 began a period of canal building by the state governments and private companies that was to last into the 1840s. By that time canals had been built connecting the major rivers with the Great Lakes and the coastal cities. Other canals joined inland cities, such as Lowell and Northhampton, Massachusetts, or Harrisburg,

Right: Workmen and officials celebrate the completion of the first transcontinental railroad. The last spike was driven on May 10, 1869, at Promontory Point, Utah.

Pennsylvania, with the Atlantic Ocean. By 1850 there were over 3,500 miles of canals in the United States. Many were poorly constructed, expensive to maintain, and subject to damage by floods and ice. But they did fill the need for water transportation where none had previously been available.

With the link to other markets, inland regions grew. These regions were now able to ship out their products to the growing national economy. They were also able to buy many eastern goods that had been too expensive before because of high freight rates.

In the middle of the century the railroad began to rival the widespread system of canals and river traffic. The first steam railway was chartered to the Baltimore and Ohio Company in 1827. Construction was slow; only 13 miles of railroad had been completed by 1830. As the problems of braking, gauge widths, engine power, and car linkage were solved, the rail network grew.

At first, state legislatures opposed the railroad. They soon began, however, to assist the growth of the railroads by giving them tax exemptions and land grants. Some railroad companies were allowed to operate banks and lotteries; others were given exclusive routes between well-traveled points. Aid to railroads between 1840 and 1853 is estimated to have exceeded $14 million in Pennsylvania alone.

The federal government, yielding to pressure from southern and western states, passed in 1850 the first in a series of laws which allowed states to grant their own land, or federally owned land, to a railroad for its right-of-way. By 1871 railroads had received about 131,350,000 acres of land, as well as loans ranging from $16,000 to $48,000 a mile depending on the difficulty of the terrain. There were over 37,000 miles of railroad completed by 1866.

As the American railroad lines moved westward, they joined cities and towns which had no natural water transportation, and they crossed the mountains that barred canals. Ultimately they linked together the sprawling regions of the country into a truly national market. Even though the first transcontinental railroad was not completed until May 1869, the rapid growth of east-west routes had tied the economic interests of the western and central states to those of the Atlantic coast, especially in the northeastern states.

On the eve of the Civil War, however, rail systems of the North and the South joined at only two points, and transfer of rolling stock was not possible because the tracks were different widths.

The first half of the nineteenth century also saw rapid development in communication. The telegraph revolutionized communication, especially in the newspaper field. Fifty thousand miles of telegraph cable had been erected by 1860. The postal system also expanded: it had 75 offices in 1790, and over 31,000 in 1866.

Regionalism

In spite of the unifying forces of improved transportation and communication, regionalism still persisted in the United States. It was intensified by developments in agriculture and manufacturing.

Agriculture in the North and the South had developed quite differently. A great many kinds of farm crops were produced in the South prior to the Civil War. Most farms were of moderate to small size. They produced corn, grain crops, livestock, cotton, and food for the local markets. The large plantations, however, contributed most to the region's income. Their staple crops of tobacco, sugar cane, rice, and cotton supplied two-thirds of American exports. The sale of these commodities abroad helped supply a giant share of capital for overall economic development of the United States.

These plantation crops were not mechanized; they required hand labor — still a scarcity in America — which was supplied by slaves. Although less than a third of Southern farmers owned any slaves, total slave population had grown to 3,950,511 by 1860.

Slaves pick cotton in Mississippi. The Southern plantations required a large amount of hand labor, which was supplied by slaves until the Civil War.

Slave quarters on a Southern plantation. Less than one-third of the Southern farmers owned slaves.

Because plantations required a large investment in land as well as slaves, and because Southern crops were subject to price drops in world markets, plantation owners often had to go into debt to financiers and exporters in the North. Some Southerners, seeing industrial wealth develop in the North and not in the South, began to believe that the North was becoming rich by taking advantage of the South.

Southerners looked to the federal government to protect their economic system, including their ownership of slaves. They also expected the government to maintain low tariffs on European imports. They feared that if the United States enacted high tariffs on foreign goods, other countries would then place high tariffs on the goods the South exported.

The North, unlike the South, sold its agricultural goods locally and nationally rather than internationally. The typical farm enterprise in the North was relatively small and was operated by the owner and his family; slavery was not necessary.

The North produced mainly corn, wheat, livestock, and cash food products. Improved machinery cut production costs, as did better transportation and liberal government land policies. Growth of urban areas in the eastern half of the country provided the North with excellent markets and led to increasing commercialization of farming. Although the wants of the farmers were relatively simple, farms became less self-sufficient. They depended on raising surpluses which they could exchange for manufactured goods and farm machinery.

There was substantial industrial development in the United States by 1860, especially in the North. The greatest employment and output were in food-processing and in other industries involved with agricultural products. Flour milling, lumber, boot and shoe manufacture, and leather goods were the most important industries. Production of iron and steel, tools, and machinery made gains, particularly in the years between 1840 and 1860. Investments in manufacturing jumped 90 percent in those two decades, and the value of industrial output rose by 85 percent. Increases in worker productivity were aided by more efficient fuel — the switch from wood to coal, and the gradual replacement of water power by steam.

The wage and factory system became firmly established. A continued shortage of skilled craftsmen gave early labor organizations bargaining power during times of prosperity. During recessions (slowdowns in economic activity) the surplus of workers and the decreased demand reduced the influence of unions.

Northern farmers and industrialists concentrated on the rapidly expanding national market. They did not sell overseas and disliked competition from foreign imports. As a result, they actively sought the very conditions the South feared, high tariffs on imports. Their economic interests, therefore, brought them into conflict with the South.

Until 1850 the new states admitted west of the Mississippi were divided equally between slave states and free states. The admission of California, Minnesota, and Oregon as free states upset the balance. With the victory of the new Republican party in 1860, and with a rising sentiment against the institution of slavery, 11 Southern states seceded from the United States. The South no longer had a voting majority in Congress, and the new president opposed slavery. The seceding states felt that their economic and social system would be in danger if they remained part of the United States.

President Lincoln held that the Union under the Constitution could not be divided, and he sought to force the South to remain. State militia attacked federal troops at Fort Sumter, South Carolina, and civil war broke out.

The War Between the States

The War Between the States strengthened and increased economic progress in the North and ended it in the South. There had already been a rising demand in the North for rail and urban construction, as well as for consumer and farm goods. The Union government's demand for ships, ammunition, uniforms, rifles, and cavalry supplies placed Northern manufacturing under even greater pressure to expand its production.

Without Southern farm products and with an army to feed, Northern agriculture was also encouraged to raise its output. Shortages of manpower forced both industry and agriculture in the North to employ more machinery. This increased the demand for capital goods. The printing of paper greenbacks to pay for war expenses increased the amount of money in the economy, which in turn stimulated Northern economic growth.

Industry in the South, on the other hand, had not developed enough to meet the demands of war. Only in the closing years of the conflict was Southern industry able to produce a large amount of arms, and it was too late to be of help. Ocean blockades and lack of export and banking facilities closed down overseas markets, severely restricting imports of necessary civilian and military goods. Poor internal transportation and a weak central government further damaged the Southern war effort.

The South did have brilliant military leadership, and it won several early battles. But the Southern

Charleston, South Carolina, in ruins. The South had to rebuild many cities and farms that were destroyed during the Civil War.

economy did not have the industrial might or organization to last out a long war. At the time of its surrender in 1865, the region had suffered vast destruction of property. It was forced to reorganize its economy without slave labor. The South experienced an almost total economic collapse, from which it took more than 50 years to recover. Victory in the North, however, laid foundations for an industrial expansion greater than any country had ever experienced.

6

Industrialization, Growth, and Instability: 1866-1929

    After the Civil War the United States experienced one of the longest and most intensive periods of economic growth in its history. Gross National Product (GNP) increased seven times in the period between the Civil War and the Great Depression. (GNP is a measure of an economy's output; it is the total value of all goods and services a country produces within one year.) From 1879 to 1919, GNP grew at an annual rate of 3.72 percent. Personal income and the standard of living also rose.

An analysis in terms of supply and demand shows that growth was brought about by increases in both supply factors and demand factors. Most important, however, was the fact that demand came to be more nearly equal to supply. This was brought about by an increase in the size of the American market. The main demand factor was the urban population, which grew from only 21 percent in the 1860s to over half the citizens by 1929, expanding the market for agriculture and manufactured products.

The supply factors within the economy also increased. The nation's resource base was enlarged by improvements in production methods, and by development of the territory west of the Mississippi River. The labor force became larger, and also more skilled and more productive through advances in mass education. Public opinion, reflected in government policies, was favorable to business and industrial enterprise.

Industrialization

The mainspring of this period was the growth of capital goods industries and the organization of large-scale production. Iron and steel production, coal mining, the petroleum industry, and the development of the electric power generator were leading factors in the surge of industrialization.

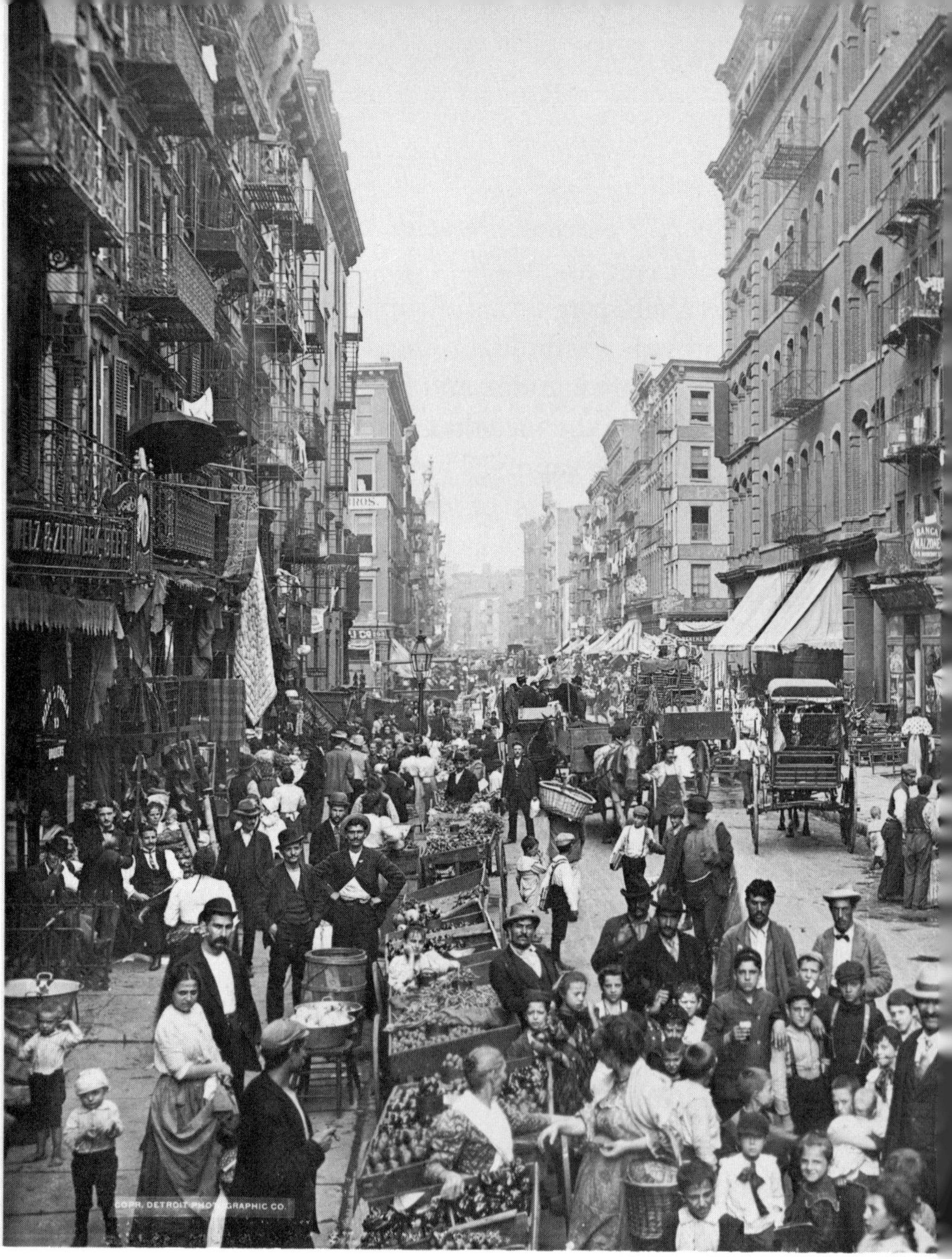
BANCA MALZONE
COPR. DETROIT PHOTOGRAPHIC CO.

Mulberry Street, New York City. The United States urban population greatly increased during the last half of the nineteenth century. This created a large demand for goods and services.

Right: Oil derricks in Kilgore, Texas, in the 1920s. The oil industry grew rapidly after the Civil War.

The value of manufactured products in the United States, $3.4 billion in 1869, rose to $24 billion by the end of 1914. In 1929 the figure had reached over $70 billion. The actual volume of manufactured goods increased 300 percent in the 30 years after 1900, while the labor force rose by only 16 percent. With these tremendous leaps in output, a higher percentage of the nation's workers, almost 40 percent, were engaged in manufacturing.

To manage large-scale operations new forms of business organization evolved. In the economic conditions before 1860, individuals or partnerships could generally raise enough capital to finance even the largest enterprises of the day. Increased use of machinery and quantity production in the decades after 1865, however, required much larger sums. The *corporation* soon replaced the partnership as the most typical form of industrial organization. Basically, a corporation is a business in which several people (stockholders) invest money. Each person owns a share of the business and receives part of the profits according to how much of the stock he owns.

Success in many industries, including the petroleum, steel, sugar, shoe machinery, copper, and railroad industries, led to the development of the *trust*, or holding company. A trust is an organization controlling several companies which turn out the same product. Trusts caused great concentrations of wealth in the hands of a few businessmen. When one corporation controls a major portion of an industry, it becomes a monopoly because it has no competition. Monopolies resulted in price discrimination against farmers and small businessmen, cut-throat competition, and careless use of the nation's resources.

The evils caused by trusts aroused public concern. The traditional *laissez-faire* policy of the federal government gradually changed; government became more involved in regulating the economy. The Interstate Commerce Commission, established in 1887, was the first of more than a dozen regulatory commissions created in the next 50 years. These commissions were given the authority to regulate prices, standards of performance, and operating practices in industries which affect the public interest — railroads, electric power, gas pipelines, radio, television, and aviation.

The Sherman Antitrust Act of 1890 and the Clayton Act of 1914 also marked a change away from

A 1900 cartoon entitled "The Trust vs. The Common People." The large trusts sit on the back of the thin and weak common people.

laissez-faire policy. With these laws the government attempted to force competition in the marketplace. They made it illegal for trusts and monopolies to fix prices, restrain trade, or discriminate against certain buyers. Enforcement was slow at first. In fact, it was directed as much at the new national trade unions as at business; organizing workers was often considered an unfair business practice.

Enactment of these laws, however, marked an important change in the role of government in the economy. Before the rise of big business, it was thought that the forces of competition alone were strong enough to keep the free enterprise and price system functioning smoothly. Most people thought that government should restrict its activities to providing police and military protection, postal service, public records, and a sound currency.

Actually, for many years before the era of big business, state and federal governments had been doing much more: they had subsidized transportation, canals, railroads, and shipping, and they had purchased, sold, and then given away vast tracts of land. The federal government had offered tariff protection to certain products and industries, allowed tax rebates, granted patents, and made loans directly to certain businesses.

Thus government participation in the economy had already been accepted in many areas in the United States. The independent commissions and the antitrust legislation, created after 1887, merely added to the government's responsibilities. Government was now charged with policing the marketplace against monopoly practices and protecting the public interests in areas where the forces of competition were inadequate.

Banking and Finance

Closely connected to the expansion of industry after the Civil War were developments in banking and finance. The United States continued to have a shortage of money and credit throughout this period. Real solutions to this problem were not developed until 1913, when the Federal Reserve System was established, creating a genuine central bank with authority to provide adequate levels of money and credit.

The Constitution had given Congress the power to coin money and the obligation to furnish a sound currency system. Congress responded by establishing a mint to turn out gold and silver coins. Because there was not much precious metal available, Congress also established a national bank to issue paper currency and to lend money at interest. The system proved good; the bank's currency generally maintained a steady value.

The charter of the national bank expired in 1811, and a Second Bank of the United States was created in 1816. This bank also issued paper money and provided credit. The charter of this bank was allowed to run out in 1836, during the administration of Andrew Jackson. General public suspicion of federal control, distrust between the officers of the central bank and other bankers, and political conflict between the director of the United States Bank and President Jackson all helped to prevent the renewal of the charter.

During the early years of the nation's development other banks were not under government control; they were privately owned and independently operated, as any other business enterprise. A few states — New York, Louisiana, Massachusetts, and Florida — after the financial panic of 1837, set up regulations governing banks under their jurisdiction, and other states began to follow their example.

After the charter of the Second Bank of the United States expired, many state banks began to issue their own paper currency. Often this currency was not backed by gold or silver, and it fell rapidly in value. The economy was filled with many kinds of paper notes; some were sound, some unsound, some of changing value.

During the War Between the States, the National Banking Acts created a system of banks controlled by the Treasury. These banks were required to have investments in government bonds to back up their deposits and paper currency. The banking laws also placed a heavy tax on state paper notes, forcing state-chartered banks to stop issuing their own currency.

A ten-dollar bill issued by the National Banking System in 1861.

The National Banking System finally established a sound national currency. The system remained satisfactory until the economy increased its demand for money and credit beyond the ability of the national banks to provide it. The basic weakness of the National Banking System was that the volume of credit was tied to the amount of government bonds issued rather than to the needs of the economy.

Financial panics and bank failures in 1873, 1893, and 1907 led to the establishment of the Federal Reserve System in 1913. The Federal Reserve has power to exert controls on the amounts of money and credit available in the economy in order to prevent severe depression or inflation. When the Federal Reserve provides large amounts of money and credit, this tends to stimulate production and prevent depression. If the money in circulation is limited by the Federal Reserve, the economy tends to slow down and thus it avoids inflation.

Agriculture

Settlement of the area west of the Mississippi continued to provide new markets and resources for the economy after the War Between the States. The farming frontier gave way to the ranching and mining frontiers. All the while new technological developments — the reaper, steel plow, twine binder, and grain harvester — enabled United States agricultural

The McCormick reaper. This invention helped United States farmers raise more agricultural products to sell at home and overseas.

resources to continue to feed and clothe a growing population as well as to supply a major quantity of the country's exports.

During the 1880s and the 1890s, however, there was considerable discontent among farmers, caused by a shift of investment to industry, falling farm prices, and high costs of tools and marketing. Farmers began to form cooperatives to reduce the cost of storing and selling their goods. During this period farmers took a more active role in politics, demanding reforms from state and federal government. After the turn of the century, the economy revived. Farm prices again rose, and industrialization speeded up.

World War I

With the outbreak of World War I, the demand by the Allied Powers for manufactured and agricultural products resulted in a further boost to American prosperity. Entry of the United States into World War I brought forth even greater demands on the economy, particularly in agriculture. In order to supply these needs, the federal government set up controls over the allocation, or distribution, of resources and output. The Food Administration set minimum prices to encourage agricultural production. The War Industries Board organized the production of defense supplies. Fuel, food, raw materials, labor, rail and ship transportation were mobilized by various federal agencies to win the war.

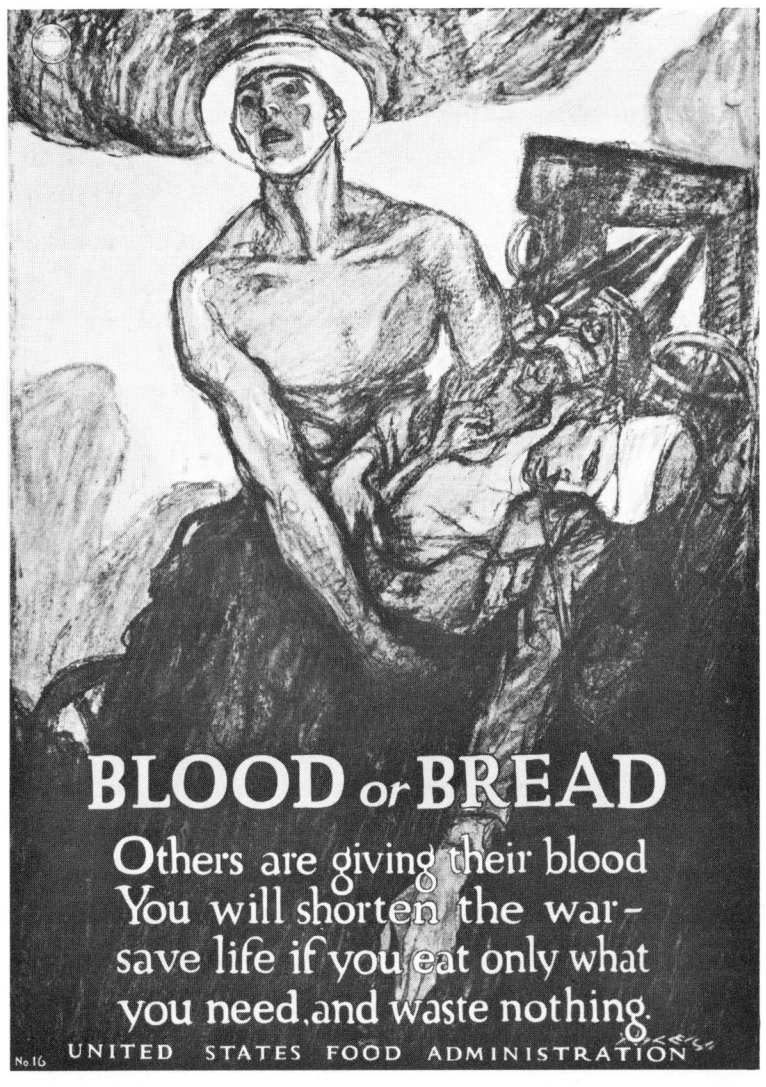

A poster issued by the United States Food Administration during World War I. The American people were encouraged not to waste food. (Chicago Historical Society)

From a purely economic standpoint the most significant effect of World War I on United States economic development was a 30 percent increase in manufacturing capacity. There was considerable inflation, but less than during the War Between the States. Labor organizations made real gains in membership and wages, and the use of government controls established a pattern for dealing with crisis conditions in an industrialized market economy.

The Roaring Twenties

The wartime boom was followed by a brief recession; military and overseas demand slacked off. As government canceled its contracts and returning soldiers increased the labor force, income was cut and the bargaining power of unions was reduced.

Business and industry, however, made a quick recovery. Average citizens held business and industry in high esteem, and government was more than friendly. The government stopped antitrust and regulatory activity almost completely during the 1920s. Concentration and consolidation of large business enterprise continued at such a rate that by 1929 the country's 200 largest non-banking corporations held assets totaling $81 billion. They owned 49 percent of corporate wealth, 38 percent of all business wealth, and 22 percent of the entire wealth of the United States.

By 1922 national prosperity had moved to a high level; the "Roaring Twenties" had arrived. Except for minor readjustments, the prosperity lasted until October 1929. Americans consumed more and better food, owned more homes and automobiles, and enjoyed higher real incomes than citizens of any other country. Building construction, electrical appliances, automobiles and trucks, synthetic rayon and plastics, radio, tobacco, and utilities sparked the good times.

A 1929 Ford. During the Roaring Twenties the automobile industry grew rapidly. More and more Americans owned cars.

All segments of the economy, however, did not participate in the prosperity. After 1923 the coal industry slipped into depression; 1,355 mines were idle by 1929. The value of textile output dropped over $400 million during the same period. Railroads and shipbuilding also went into decline, as foreign trade decreased and the volume of domestic freight and passengers began to be shared by trucks, buses, and automobiles. Shoe manufacturing and leather goods never gained their earlier levels. Grain and liquor sales fell when Prohibition (the prevention of the sale and distribution of alcoholic beverages) began in 1920.

Of all the depressed industries, the most seriously affected was agriculture. People left the farms at a rapid rate — 1,201,000 between 1920 and 1930. The output of agricultural products was increased by greater use of machinery and greater productivity of farm workers. At the same time, however, the demand for agricultural products declined. After 1920 foreign markets became smaller; diet preferences changed (more protein, fewer carbohydrates); silk and rayon were substituted for cotton and flax; and population growth was slower. All these factors combined to reduce the market for farm-produced goods.

The McNary-Haugen bill, proposed in Congress in 1924, would have raised farm prices at home and lowered prices on farm exports. At first Congress failed to pass this bill, and then President Coolidge vetoed it in 1927 and 1928. In 1929 Congress enlarged

Senator Charles L. McNary of Oregon, and Representative Gilbert N. Haugen of Iowa. These men proposed a bill in Congress which would have provided relief for American farmers in the 1920s.

tariff protection for farmers and provided increased credit for farmers. But these measures failed to bring this part of the economy out of the doldrums.

Organized labor lost strength after the war; unions had a million and a half fewer members in 1929 than they had in 1920. The dominant pro-business philosophy of the times led to company-sponsored unions. The influence of unions was further reduced by their failure to organize the new mass-production industries.

Signs of economic weakness were becoming more numerous by the end of the decade, even though businessmen were predicting continued prosperity. Home building reached a peak in 1925 and declined steadily thereafter. Automobile sales fell off beginning in 1927, and unemployment in many heavy industries became noticeable in 1928.

Most industries continued to produce at a rapid rate, and consumers were encouraged to buy more through increased advertising. Consumers could not buy all of the products turned out by industry, however, without borrowing; they used installment credit, buying "on time," to finance their purchases. Total consumer credit rose from $2 billion in 1924 to some $3.5 billion in mid-1929. Such a large amount of borrowing weakened the economy. Individuals borrowed too far into the future, and when economic activity slowed down, they were left without means to pay their debts.

As factories continued production, consumers were eventually unable to buy everything, and sales began to decline. This, in turn, forced factories to reduce their output and discharge workers, creating unemployment. With greater unemployment, fewer goods were purchased, and so production was reduced even further. This process, as it continued, caused a large drop in the economy's overall production, employment, and income.

One reason that consumers were unable to buy all

the goods being produced was that they were not receiving enough money. The profits businesses made were not returned to the wage earner. Because ownership of most corporations was concentrated in the hands of a few people, upper income groups received most of the business profits throughout the decade. Eighty percent of all corporate dividends went to the top 5 percent of the population.

Because wealthy people need to spend only a small portion of their income on goods and services, less and less money went back into demand for consumer products. Money from business profits instead sought outlets in investment and stock market speculation (buying a stock in the expectation that its price will rise and produce a profit).

Many of the weak spots which developed in the United States economy during the twenties were hidden by continually rising prices on the stock market. Soaring values attracted experienced investors and amateurs alike. Purchasing securities seemed to be a vote of confidence in the economy and a way of insuring continued expansion.

The value of a security was figured on the basis of how much it would earn during the year. Traditionally, a stock's price was 10 times the expected per share earnings for that year. In 1929, however, some popular issues were selling at 50 times this amount. This created an unrealistic value for stocks; their price increased much faster than the actual productivity of the economy. In fact, stock prices rose rapidly at the same time that the economy was declining. From March to September 1929, United States Steel shares rose from $138 to $279; American Telephone and Telegraph jumped from $179 to $355.

Widespread speculation was encouraged by many factors: money could be borrowed at low interest rates; brokers readily gave loans for a large percentage of the price of the stock; and the government paid off its World War I bonds, increasing the amount of money in public hands by $800 million a year.

International economic conditions also became unsteady during the 1920s. The United States continually exported many more goods than it imported; high American tariffs made it impossible for European nations to export their products to this country. Foreign governments began to enact trade restrictions discriminating against American products. In order to keep money at home, foreign governments also restricted investments; in late 1928 the American stock market was weakened by withdrawal of foreign investment funds. These restrictions did not give foreign countries enough income, however, to pay off their wartime loans from the United States.

The Great Depression

The bubble of prosperity burst shortly after 10 A.M. on Tuesday, October 29, 1929. By the end of the

STOCK PRICES SLUMP $14,000,000,000 IN NATION-WIDE STAMPEDE TO UNLOAD; BANKERS TO SUPPORT MARKET TODAY

Sixteen Leading Issues Down $2,893,520,108; Tel. & Tel. and Steel Among Heaviest Losers

A shrinkage of $2,893,520,108 in the open market value of the shares of sixteen representative companies resulted from yesterday's sweeping decline on the New York Stock Exchange.

The lead article from the New York Times on the morning of October 29, 1929. It reports that millions of shares of stock had been sold. The bankers were expecting to rescue the market on the 29th, but prices dropped completely and finally that morning.

PREMIER ISSUES HARD HIT

Unexpected Torrent of Liquidation Again Rocks Markets.

DAY'S SALES 9,212,800

Nearly 3,000,000 Shares Are Traded In Final Hour—The Tickers Lag 167 Minutes.

NEW RALLY SOON BROKEN

day 16,410,030 shares had been sold, and the average price of 50 leading stocks had fallen nearly $40. Collapse of the building boom, decline of consumer goods and investment, heavy personal and business indebtedness, and unfavorable international developments had undermined the economy months before the drop in stock prices registered the change. A speculative fever had continued to push prices up. As the value of securities fell, loans and collateral became worthless. With so many investors seeking to turn their stocks into cash, the people who did have money to

75

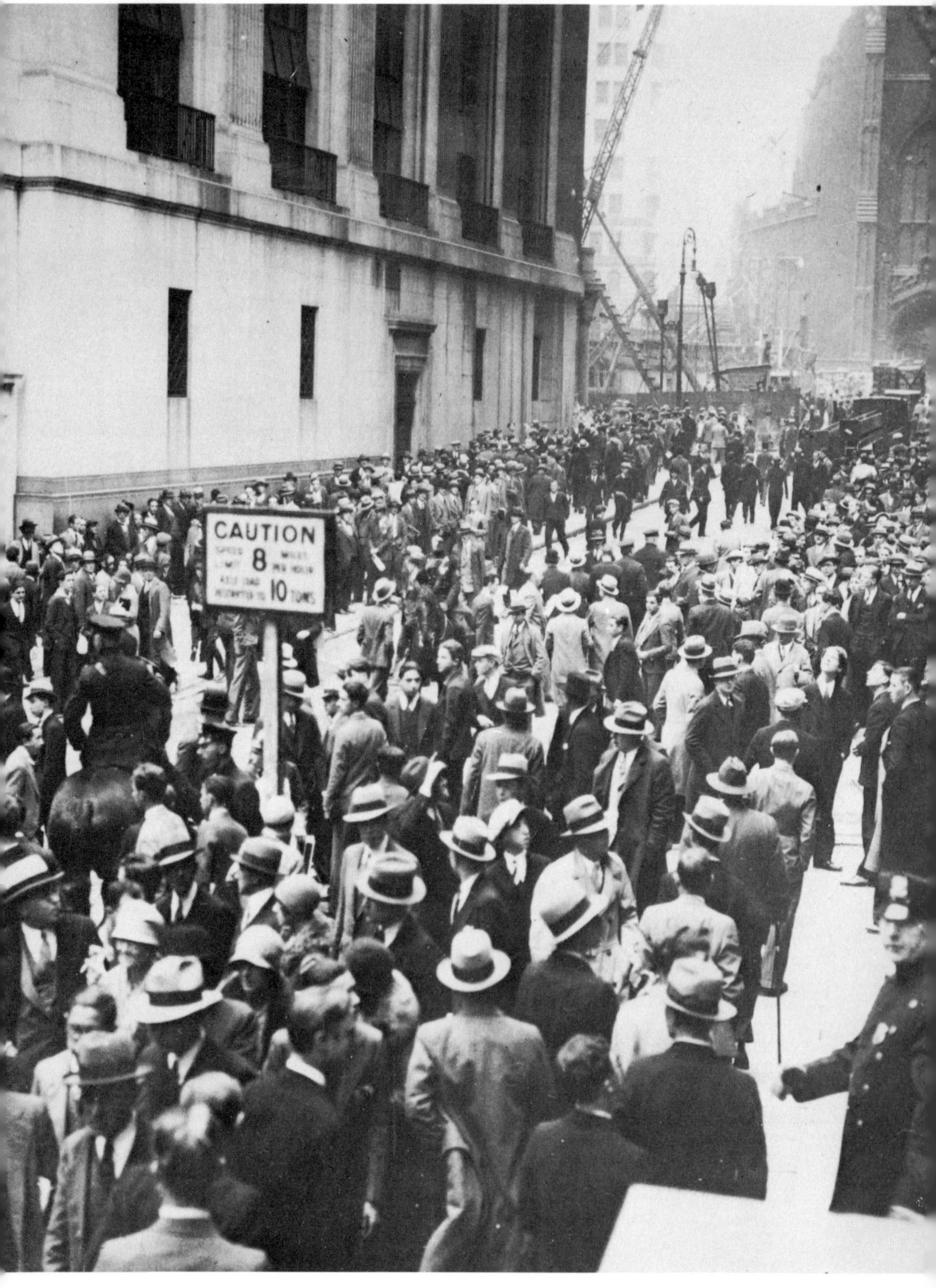
CAUTION
8
10

invest waited for the prices to fall even lower. Because no one wanted to buy stocks, their prices continued to fall rapidly, and the Great Depression began.

The depression raised some serious questions about an economy which had experienced more than a century of extraordinary, if uneven, growth. In 1929 the economy was in depression and stagnation even though productive resources were in greater supply than ever before. Even the long-time shortages of capital and skilled labor had been overcome. But the economy now suffered from low levels of purchasing power (due to widespread unemployment and lack of demand), and also from insufficient capital investment to provide jobs.

A broad analysis of the depression shows that by 1929 the ability of the American economy to produce goods and services had become much greater than the capability of the marketplace to absorb the output. Supply had exceeded demand. Business concentration, the formation of trusts and monopolies, and a *laissez-faire* policy by government had led to a decline of competition, raising prices. Profits and dividends had flowed to upper income groups and therefore failed to provide enough purchasing power to stimulate consumer demand and higher levels of investment. Unregulated credit and unrealistic speculation in the stock market contributed to economic instability.

Left: Crowds gather on Wall Street after the stock market crash.

7

Development of American Capitalism: 1929 to the Present

The American economy had experienced the effects of business cycles (alternating periods of prosperity and recession) throughout its history. Recessions had followed wars and periods of low farm prices. In 1837, 1857, 1873, and 1893, they were accompanied by financial panics; private citizens and investors lost faith in the economy and withdrew their funds from banks and the stock markets. There had been times of inflation too, during major wars mainly, but also in years of high prosperity in the mid-1820s, 1880s, and just after the turn of the twentieth century.

An unemployed man sells an apple for a nickel. During the Great Depression, many men sold apples for money to feed their families.

The depression that followed the stock market crash of 1929 was by far the most severe experienced in the United States. Unfortunately, the historic ways of handling recessions or depressions were geared to a simpler, less interdependent, economic system: technology had outdistanced the rate of institutional change. When depression struck, businessmen expected the economy to recover automatically, without government assistance. But this traditional method of recovery was too weak. Worst of all, the wage-earning population had no cushion of security to protect them; there were no institutions to provide unemployment compensation or welfare. Unemployed workers faced actual starvation.

By 1932 over 5,000 banks had failed, wiping out the savings and deposits of their customers. Farm prices, already low after a decade of decline, dropped by an additional 66 percent in three years. The number of business failures increased by more than 50 percent, and business profits almost disappeared. Corporations as a whole lost $3 billion in 1932. In the heavily concentrated steel industry, prices declined only 20 percent, but production was reduced by 80 percent. Average weekly wages in manufacturing, $25 in 1925, sank to $17 in 1932. The number of unemployed soared.

Estimates of the number of unemployed workers range from 12 to 20 million. The lower figure was about one-fourth of the labor force. Output of goods and services fell by 30 percent; industrial production was halved. By 1938 the total income lost because of the depression was 133.1 billion dollars. The economic loss was great, but the human suffering was unmatched in our previous history.

President Hoover's anti-depression program did not greatly improve conditions; it suffered from its small scale and from the fact that federal government had never before attempted to bring the economy out of collapse. High tariffs established by the Smoot-Hawley Act attempted to decrease competition from foreign imports. They only succeeded, however, in reducing United States exports, as other countries raised their tariffs. High taxes, levied in an attempt to balance the budget, also made matters worse by reducing demand; consumers had less money to spend. Loans to industry through the Reconstruction Finance Corporation helped, but they were too slow in taking effect.

The New Deal

The government's failure to provide relief measures or to get people back to work as the depression continued into 1932 caused voters to turn to new leadership. Franklin D. Roosevelt promised change in the form of a New Deal.

Franklin Delano Roosevelt speaks to the country over the radio. His New Deal programs helped to get the economy going again.

The New Deal program was largely experimental at first, attacking symptoms and seeking causes, but ultimately it did change the outdated government institutions. In the first three months of 1933 Congress gave to the new president broad powers to adjust the country's money and banking system, and to set up programs to assist agriculture and industry. The Agricultural Adjustment Act paid farmers for not raising their usual amounts of cotton, hogs, wheat, and other staple commodities. This was done in order to reduce the supply of farm products and thereby raise farm prices. A far-reaching National Industrial Recovery Act required various industries to draw up codes to regulate wages, hours, prices, and output.

Although these acts were later declared unconstitutional by the Supreme Court, they set the mood of the new administration and marked a change in government policy. The government would now establish minimum prices for agricultural products to raise farm incomes; it would encourage standard wages and hours, and it would ask business to cooperate in handling the crisis.

To help business recover, the New Deal provided loans and credit. Sometimes it insured companies against the risks of expanding during recession by agreeing to repay loans if the business failed. For individuals, government policy sought first to provide relief, then jobs and income. When individuals again were earning money, this would stimulate the demand for consumer goods. It was hoped that if government "primed" the investment and consumption "pump" in this manner, the economy would recover its natural activity.

Congress voted several billions of dollars to provide emergency relief and set up agencies to create jobs for the unemployed. The Works Progress Administration (WPA), the Public Works Administration (PWA), the National Youth Administration (NYA), and the Civilan Conservation Corps (CCC) were part of the "alphabet soup" agencies created by government policies in the 1930s.

New Deal programs provided aid for the homeowner and the farmer, credit to prevent foreclosures on mortgages, insurance plans to protect bank depositors, and a commission to regulate the stock market. Programs for the establishment of old age pensions and unemployment compensation were also created, along with a new income tax law which taxed upper income groups most heavily.

The dollar was devalued; it was declared to be worth a smaller amount of gold, so that it had less value in relation to the currencies of other nations. This lowered the price of American products in the world market, which stimulated export trade, thereby increasing the demand for United States products.

Organized labor became stronger as a result of the New Deal. The National Labor Relations Act of 1935 guaranteed the right to collective bargaining and the freedom to organize workers. Moreover, public attitude toward unions changed. Wage earners realized that their interests were closer to those of labor than management or property owners. The change in public attitude reflected the fact that more people were becoming employees. In 1890 more than half the labor force was self-employed, but after 1929 more than half the labor force was on someone's payroll.

Although the New Deal failed to achieve total prosperity (which came only with the beginning of World War II), it did represent action, a vigorous attack on the problems created by depression. The aim of the New Deal was not to make a socialistic economic system (putting control in the hands of the government), but to prop up the capitalistic system. The many regulations and controls were almost without exception *indirect;* property remained in private hands, and the market's influence was still the strongest force, although the limits of its operation were narrower.

Economic conditions were much improved 10 years after the New Deal began. Farm prices were up 22 percent, and agricultural income had almost doubled from the 1933 low. Weekly wages had climbed back to $23.86 in the manufacturing industries. About four million of the unemployed had gone back to work. No banks had failed since 1934, and foreclosures of home and farm mortgages were fewer than in the 1920s. Real wages (the value of wages after compensating for price inflation) rose 20 percent overall, and industrial production increased 60 percent between 1933 and the end of the decade. The national debt grew from about $16 billion in 1929 to $34.9 billion on the eve of World War II, as the government spent money within the economy in order to raise demand for goods and services.

Under the New Deal the federal government assumed responsibility for the economic welfare of individuals and the economy as a whole. Its policies developed a "mixed economy," one with primarily private ownership and control, with some areas of government regulation. Although many Americans disliked increased government control, others were encouraged by the results. Perhaps the most important contribution to recovery made by the New Deal was that it restored confidence in the political and economic system and focused on the real resources of growth that were present.

World War II

The entry of the United States into World War II in 1941 began a spectacular buildup of productive capacity. The defense industries had experienced almost three years of slow revival before 1941, but war demands brought rapid expansion. Total output of industrial products in 1943 was over three times as great as in 1939; by 1944 GNP was 70 percent above the 1939 level.

Government improved upon the emergency wartime controls pioneered in World War I; it established a wide variety of agencies and boards to coordinate the increased production, helping factories to turn out defense products and distributing the products among those who needed them. By placing a limit on wages and prices, and by rationing food products, government prevented runaway inflation. Consumer prices rose only 4.2 percent between April 1943 through August 1945. Government, especially the armed forces, was the economy's biggest customer. At the peak of the war, government expenditures consumed almost 50 percent of the record $220 billion GNP.

Wartime was a prosperous period for the labor force as well as for industry. Wages doubled over their 1939 level. Overtime pay, added to the rise in wages, caused an actual increase of 53 percent. Labor unions, after receiving favorable legislation during the 1930s, became larger and more powerful during World War II. Union leaders played an important role in the war effort, and union membership between 1939 and 1945 jumped from 9 million to over 15 million. Mass-production workers had joined the newly formed Congress of Industrial Organizations (CIO) at a rapid rate after its founding in 1936, and by the end of World War II, labor union membership was about equally divided between the CIO and the older American Federation of Labor.

The Postwar Period

Explosion of the atomic bomb in August of 1945 did more than end the war; it opened the way to a new energy source and a concern over the transition to peacetime.

After the war it appeared that the economy might again undergo a recession. During the first six months after the war 70,000 government contracts were canceled, and 2.5 million workers were discharged. Wartime controls were allowed to lapse in June 1946, and in a short time prices on some consumer items rose as much as 25 percent. Rising prices resulted from increased demand for goods and services, a demand stimulated by a wartime baby boom, large amounts of personal savings, and high personal income.

Fearing greater unemployment, and a return to recession conditions, Congress passed the Employment Act of 1946. This legislation, supported by both major political parties, gave the federal government the responsibility of promoting high levels of employment, maintaining price stability, and assuring a healthy rate of growth. Thus the Employment Act made law the general philosophy of the New Deal; it committed government to include economic growth and development as part of its function.

The immediate postwar years were characterized by a wave of prosperity and inflation. Growth was aided by the need to satisfy long pent up consumer demand and by the expansion of new industries created by the war effort — electronics, plastics, television, and synthetic fabrics.

To counteract the effects of inflation after the war, unions led a drive for higher wages, which resulted in a record number of strikes — 4,985 in 1946 alone. Citizens were inconvenienced and angered by this show of power, and Congress passed the Taft-Hartley Act of 1947 regulating collective bargaining and strike activities of labor unions. The Landrum-Griffin Act,

The United Nations General Assembly in session. After World War II the United States actively supported this organization, hoping that it would help keep peace among nations.

passed in 1959, policed the internal operations of unions. Labor, like other parts of the economy which upset the popular concept of acceptable market behavior, came under the regulation of the laws.

After World War I, the United States had refused to join the League of Nations, an international organization formed with the hope of keeping world peace. But following World War II, the United States became a member of the United Nations and took an active part in international affairs. In the late 1940s,

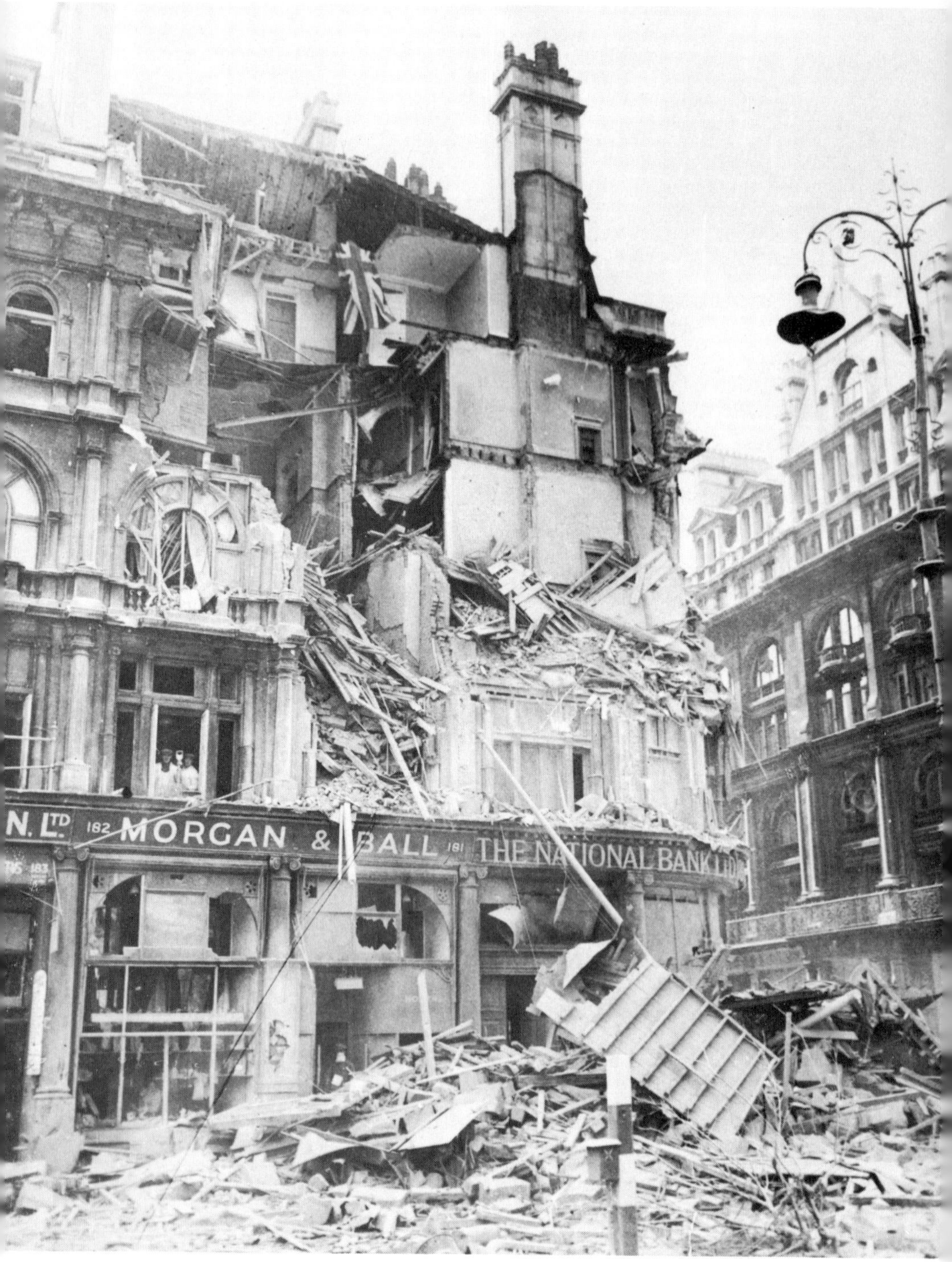
N. LTD
182 MORGAN & BALL
181 THE NATIONAL BANK LTD

Left: A London bank building in ruins after World War II bombings. The United States, under the Marshall Plan, gave aid to England and other European countries for reconstruction after the war.

under the Marshall Plan, the United States participated in relief and reconstruction in Western Europe by providing aid to countries damaged by the war.

The Marshall Plan led to a long range policy of aid to the underdeveloped nations of the world. The reasons for this policy were partly economic — to insure markets, sources of raw materials, and active recovery of trading partners. They were also partly political — to stem the growing influence of the Soviet Union in Europe and Asia.

The attempt to contain communism led to the cold war in Europe, fighting in Korea, and 10 years later, war in Viet Nam. The international responsibilities of defending the free world required rearmament. The tremendous American productive capacity of World War II, which had been expanded by postwar civilian demands, was increased even more. The United States economy began to do what no other economy had attempted to do before, satisfy its domestic consumer needs while at the same time maintaining a vast program of military defense and foreign economic assistance. The effort pushed the Gross National Product to record levels, caused a mild inflation, and added $17 billion to the national debt, which rose to $286 billion by 1960.

Economic growth of the United States in the decade of the 1950s was stimulated by technological advances and increasing research carried out by business and government. New industries sparked the advance — atomic energy, jet aircraft, prepackaged and frozen foods, construction materials, and petrochemicals (chemicals derived from oil).

Farm prices reached their highest peak during the war only to fall in the years after. The federal government began to support farm prices. It bought supplies of agricultural products when their prices fell below minimum levels, creating a scarcity, and causing prices to rise. Even so, farm population continued to decline.

The most disturbing characteristic of the period was a series of slight but sharp recessions in 1953, 1957, and again in 1959. Each of these fluctuations was accompanied by steadily rising unemployment figures reaching an annual average of 6.8 percent of the civilian labor force by 1958.

These events coincided with a slowdown in the rate of the economy's growth. The economy's output rose on the average a little less than 4.7 percent a year from 1921 to 1929. Between 1947 and 1957 the rate was somewhat less, but still a respectable 3.9 percent. After 1957, and until 1962, the growth of output slipped to just under 3 percent a year.

Huge amounts of federal spending, and programs such as the building of an interstate highway system, created some demand for goods and services within the economy. But in spite of this demand, the economy continued to lag. This occurred at a time when the Soviet Union and the countries of Western Europe were growing at a rate twice that of the United States. The weakness of the American economy in relation to these countries set off a debate over the policies needed to stimulate economic growth.

The New Frontier

In the presidential campaign of 1960, John F. Kennedy promised "to get the country moving again." The economic policies of his administration, the New Frontier, concentrated on the symptoms of slow growth; it began to increase the level of demand within the economy.

The federal government increased its expenditures on housing and urban redevelopment, giving loans and credit to regions which were less prosperous than the rest of the country. It expanded the national aeronautics and space program to aim at landing men on the moon before 1970.

The government not only increased its own demand in the economy, but it also stimulated private demand. It began to reduce unemployment through a program of manpower retraining and by increasing job opportunities. The government established tax incentives (favorable tax rates) on money spent for industrial development. This channeled business savings into expenditures for new plants and equipment (which also had the impact of providing jobs), and thereby introduced more modern capital goods into production. When business used better equipment and more modern methods of production, the result was a greater efficiency of resource use. The growth rate of the economy after 1963 rose above the historical average to a little over 4 percent, then 5 percent, through 1969.

A man repairs a machine that operates other machines. Advanced methods of production helped the United States increase its growth rate after 1963.

The pressures of rapid growth reduced unemployment to about 3.6 percent in 1968 and brought an inflationary trend; too large a demand within an economy will cause a rise in prices. The government in 1968 took deliberate steps to cool off the economy, although they were somewhat late to solve the problem completely.

The first restraint on the economy took the form of an income surtax. The enactment of a surtax requires businesses and individuals to pay their regular income tax plus a certain percentage of that amount. A surtax gives taxpayers less money to spend and thereby tends to reduce the demand level in the economy.

This use of a surtax marked the establishment of tax policy as a major tool both to push and to slow the economic growth process in the United States. The Revenue Act of 1964 had cut personal and corporate taxes in order to stimulate demand and encourage growth; the surtax in 1968 sought to reduce demand and thereby curtail inflation. The surtax was renewed in 1969 as inflation continued.

The government also attempted to reduce demand in the late 1960s by discouraging excess private investment within the economy. This was done through an adjustment in monetary policy; the Federal Reserve reduced the amount of money available, which raised interest rates on investment capital.

The surtax and the raise of interest rates were less effective in changing economic trends than the

This cartoon shows that the enemy, inflation, can easily win against anti-inflation measures that are too little and too late.

tax cut of 1964. One reason for this was the tendency for business to concentrate into larger units. Concentration began in the last quarter of the nineteenth century and continued with the merger movement (companies buying or joining other firms) in the 1950s and the turn to *conglomerates* in the 1960s. Conglom-

Right: Army men in training at Fort Lee, Virginia. Continued military spending by the government is one reason that anti-inflation measures have not been successful.

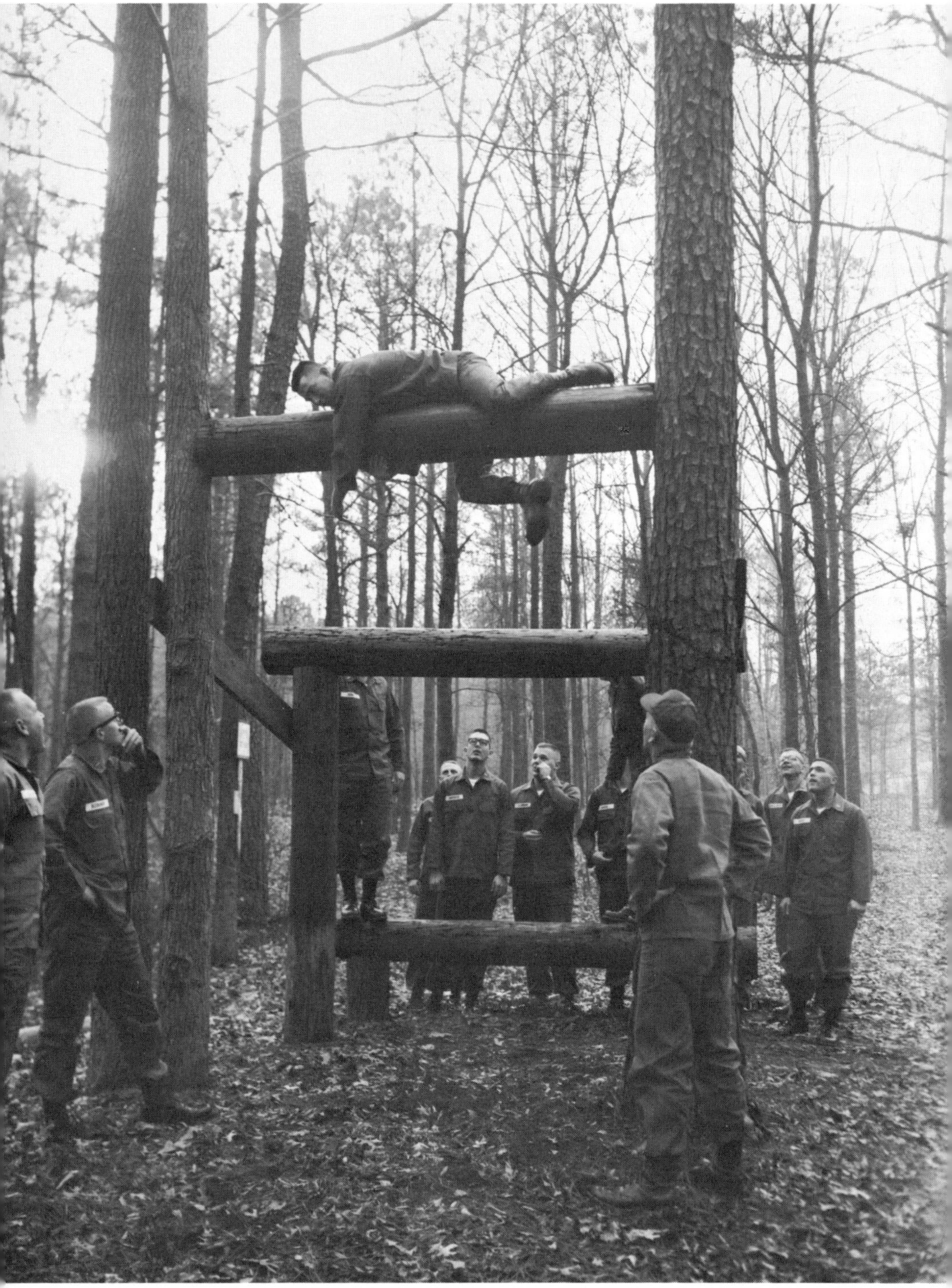

Right: An Apollo moon rocket. Space, like the American continents 400 years ago, is an unexplored area, filled with exciting prospects.

erates are giant organizations embodying many different kinds of products, controlled by a single corporation. Conglomerates have sources of investment capital from the various companies they own, so that their investment is not readily cut back by higher interest rates in the general economy.

Another reason for the ineffectiveness of the anti-inflation measures in the late 1960s was that the government continued its spending, on the war in Viet Nam, on defense, and on programs designed to solve some of the problems within the United States industrial economy. Cities which had sparked industrialization and past waves of construction were beginning to wear out and need rebuilding. A population exceeding 200 million persons required more housing, schools, recreational facilities, and medical care than ever before. In conditions of economic plenty, the government launched a program to share the output more equally by seeking to eliminate poverty and build a "Great Society."

These demands on an economy, even one so productive as that of the United States, are enough to cause strain. The challenge ahead is clearly outlined by the events of the last 200 years. How can the American economy organize its resources to meet the economic needs of the time and continue to preserve individual freedom and the drive for material well-being, which have sparked past growth and development?

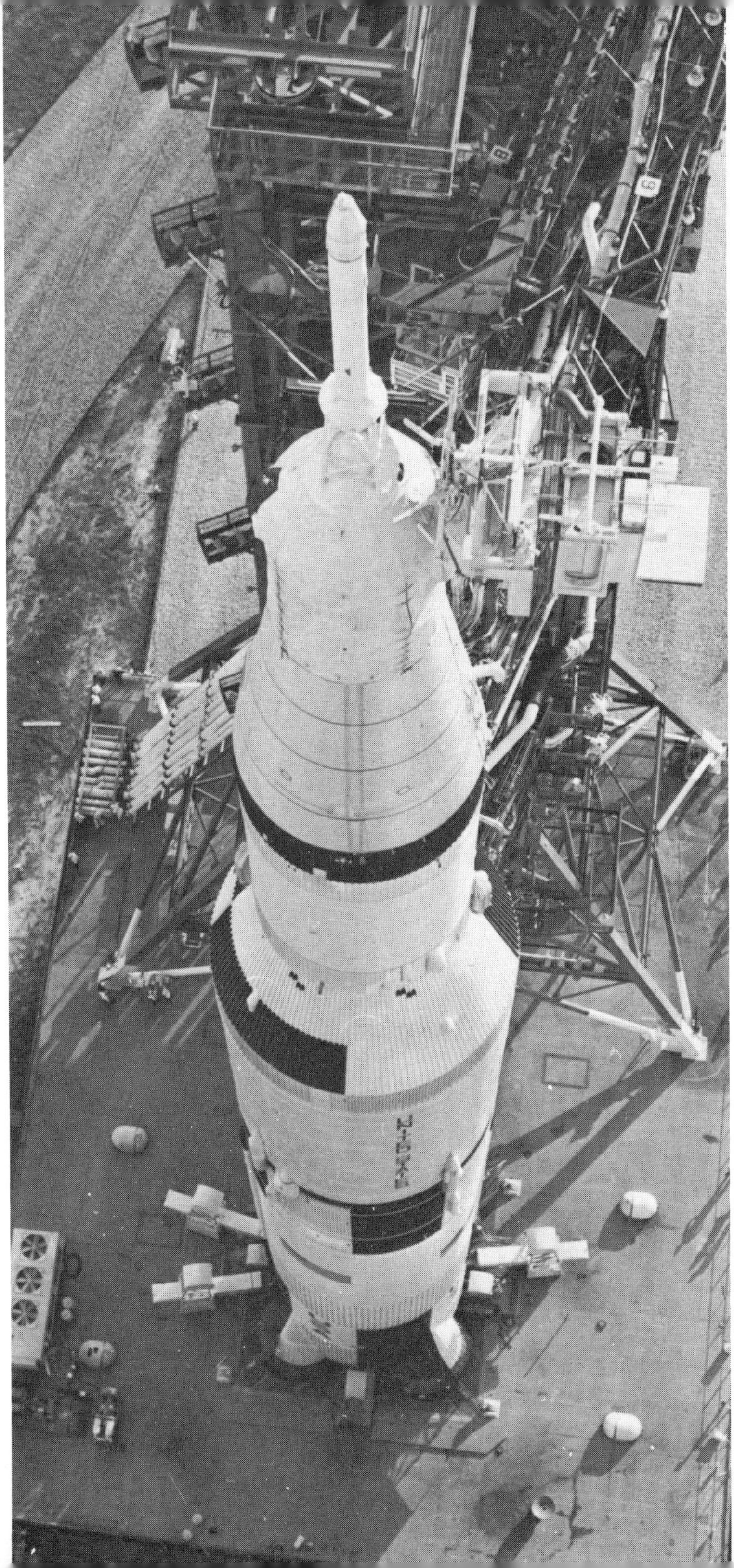

The American economy has thus far been able to provide for its citizens a richer material life than any other country. It has made it possible for men to walk on the moon, and it will be sending men on to further space exploration, much as the nation states of Western Europe sent men to the New World 350 years ago. The Europeans had, as the United States continues to have, unfinished work at home. Yet European exploration provided the mainspring for the growth of the American economy. A look at the development in our own past makes speculation about future growth all the more exciting.

Glossary

capital — An economic resource or factor of production. Money and its productive use.

conglomerate — A large business organization controlling unrelated enterprises. This type of corporation became popular in the mid-1960s.

corporation — A form of business organization in which many investors provide capital for large-scale operations.

entrepreneurship — The ability to manage a business organization and combine economic factors profitably.

indentured servants — Men who agreed to work several years for the man who paid their passage to North America.

laissez-faire (leh-say-fair) — The French term applied to minimum government regulation of business activity.

mercantilism — An economic policy which attempted to create an export balance of trade in order to build up a nation's wealth.

technology — The methods of production within an economy. Advances in this area speed a country's economic growth or progress.

trust — An organization which controls many companies within a particular industry.

Index

agriculture, colonial, 28-31
   nineteenth century, 65-66
   Northern, 49-50, 51
   Southern, 46-49
   twentieth century, 70-71, 80, 84, 92
Articles of Confederation, 36-37
banking, 62-64
Bill of Rights, 38
canals, 42-44
capitalism, 14, 38-39, 84-85
Civil War, 50-53
conglomerates, 96
Constitution of the United States, 38-39, 62
corporations, 58
Employment Act of 1946, 87
feudalism, 14-15, 21-22
Great Depression, 13, 72-73, 77, 79
immigration, 22-23
indentured servants, 24
industry, colonial, 31
   nineteenth century, 55, 58-62
   Northern, 49-50
   Revolutionary War, 35-36, 38
   Southern, 51-53
   twentieth century, 85, 91-94
inflation, 64, 68, 86-88, 95-96, 98

labor unions, 28, 50, 71, 83-84, 86, 88-89
laissez-faire policy, 59-61, 77
McNary-Haugen bill, 70-71
Marshall Plan, 91
mercantilism, 17-18
money, 28, 51, 62-64
monopoly, 58-62
New Deal, 81-85
New Frontier, 93-94
Prohibition, 70
railroads, 44-46
Revolutionary War, 34-36
roads, 41-42
slavery, 24, 26, 47-48, 50, 53
stock market, 73-77
surtax, 95
trade, 28, 30-31, 38, 50, 74, 80, 83
United Nations, 89, 91
Viet Nam, 91, 98
World War I, 66, 78
World War II, 66, 78

the author . . .

Kenneth H. Smith is an associate professor of economics at Hunter College, City University of New York. He has been an economic consultant to private firms and also several United Nations agencies. Professor Smith received both his bachelor's and his master's degrees from Southern Methodist University and his Ph.D. from the University of Oklahoma. Dr. Smith is coauthor of *Economics*, an economics text for college students.